Tasty Healthy Easy LCHF
Kosher Low-Carb Cooking for Beginners

Dina David

Tasty Healthy Easy LCHF
Kosher Low-Carb Cooking for Beginners

Dina David

Senior Editors & Producers: Contento de Semrik
Editor: Sybil Kaplan
Photographer: Tal Almog
Design: Liliya Lev Ari
Cover Design: Liliya Lev Ari

Copyright © 2015 by Contento de Semrik
and Dina David

All rights reserved. No part of this book may be translated,
reproduced, stored in a retrieval system or transmitted,
in any form or by any means, electronic, photocopying,
recording or otherwise, without prior permission in writing from the
author and publisher.

ISBN: 978-965-550-352-4

International sole distributor:
Contento de Semrik
22 Isserles Street, 67014, Tel Aviv, Israel
Semrik10@gmail.com
www.Semrik.com

Tasty Healthy Easy LCHF
Kosher Low-Carb Cooking for Beginners
Dina David

Table of Contents:

Why did I write this cookbook? 7
Thanks 8
My story 9
What is LCHF? Diet or lifestyle? 11
Why should I eat LCHF? 13
    What's in our food? 15
    What do I eat on LCHF? What do I not eat? 17
    How much should I eat? When should I eat? 19
LCHF for vegetarians 20
Do you want to know more about LCHF? 21
Useful kitchen tools 22
Ingredients 23

Breakfast 31
Porridge 32
Coconut pancakes 33
Egg milk latte 34
Shakshouka 36

Lunch/Dinner 41
Cheese & herb pie 42
Cheese and tuna casserole dish 44
Chicken drumsticks in curry 46
Stuffed chicken 48
Chuck in wine 50
"Almost goulash" stew 52
Roast in pesto 55
Minced meat in 3 different ways, at least 56
    1. Burgers 57
    2. Meatloaf 58
    3. Meat sauce 60
Swedish cabbage pudding 62
Simplest salmon ever 63
Tuna patties 64
Upside-down pizza 67

Side Dishes 71
Schmaltz and grebnitz 72
A stewed side dish 73
Cauliflower rice 74
Egg noodles 76
Green beans in tomato sauce 80
Herb butter 82
Mashed cauliflower 84
Quick mayo 86
Salads 88
   1. Spinach salad 90
   2. Cabbage & root salad 92
Onion casserole dish 94

Snacks 99
Eggs 100
Cheeses 102
   1. Tzaziki-like cheese dip 104
   2. Blue cheese balls 105

Desserts & Candy 109
Ice cream 110
Coconut pudding with apple sauce 112
Chocolate fun 114
   1. Chocolate bars with nuts and other goodies 115
   2. Ganache 116
   3. Ice chocolate 117
Chocolate spread 118

Breads, Cakes, Cookies 123
Very quick breakfast rolls 124
Auntie's cheesecake 126
Chocolate cookies 128
Cinnamon cookies 129
Oopsies 130
Pie crust - sweet 132
Pie crust - savory 133
Za'atar bread 134

WHY DID I WRITE THIS COOKBOOK?

Yet another cookbook? Why?

When I first tell people about LCHF, Low Carb High (Healthy) Fat, a lot of them, even experienced cooks, get confused. Many times I hear, "how do I make schnitzel without bread crumbs," or "what should I eat for breakfast if I can't have cornflakes?" This cookbook is for them.

Then there are those who very much would like to cook healthy but think it takes a lot of time; or maybe they feel they don't know what truly healthy is. This cookbook is for them too.

And then there are those who just don't know how to cook at all. This cookbook is for all those as well.

And it is also for those to whom kosher cooking is important; there are many "low carb" recipes available elsewhere, but mostly they are not kosher.

So whatever your reason, "Tasty, Healthy, Easy LCHF: Kosher Low-Carb Cooking for Beginners" will try to encompass most of the above.

Enjoy!

And a bonus: All LCHF recipes are automatically kosher for Passover!

THANKS

A lot of people have encouraged me and helped me to write this cookbook - from my kids to total strangers - and I'm very happy, and lucky, to have this army of support. Thank you all!

But there are two persons, in particular, who I would like to point out: my sister, Ewa, whose ideas, more than once, have made me think of new routes and possibilities. Thank you, Sis!

And last, but definitely not least, my dear best ever partner in life, Yossi, who stands sometimes beside me, sometimes behind me, and who always supports and encourages me and my sometimes crazy ideas. In general and specifically, he is my best friend, thinking partner, and the best thing that ever happened to me. I love you!

MY STORY

I was born and raised in Stockholm, Sweden, and I've been interested in nutrition for as long as I can remember. I took a few courses on the subject at Uppsala University, and I have always enjoyed cooking, baking, and especially, innovating in the kitchen.

After moving to Israel in 1985, I worked in a variety of fields, ranging from hotels to high-tech, until I decided to become a professional pastry chef. My dream was to open my own café and serve authentic Swedish specialties. During that time, since 1985, I also got married, gave birth to a couple of kids, and found, like most women, that I had managed to gain a few extra kilos along the way.

Naturally, with my knowledge of nutrition and cooking, I thought I knew about sensible eating and how to lose weight. So I ate "healthy-whole-grains," "fruit-'n-vegetables," and "low-fat-everything." I also drank plenty of water, exercised on and off, and, mostly, I felt well. But I didn't shed those extra kilos. And my doctor started urging me to pay attention to my cholesterol and blood sugar levels.

Then, by chance, I came across information about the LCHF diet. It sounded too good to be true. The Swedish LCHF lifestyle would allow me to eat butter and brie without counting calories, and even have a piece of chocolate and drink a glass of wine from time to time, as long as I gave up bread, pasta, and potatoes.

Being the curious person I am, I began researching the concept and its basis. Very quickly, I discovered that this nutritional approach is remarkably well-grounded, evolutionarily and biochemically, and it overturned every "fact" that I had grown up believing! I was thrilled to eat tasty foods that I love, and it didn't take long before I noticed that I was also feeling much better and more energetic than I had in a long time. Thus, I began my personal health revolution and my new professional direction.

Since then, I have been fully involved in the LCHF lifestyle, helping others to regain their optimum health and weight. I also went to Sweden to study and became an LCHF nutritionist.

I decided to write this cookbook when I saw the many beginners' questions about LCHF cooking. I hope this book will guide you when starting the LCHF journey to live a truly healthy and tasty life, as well as inspire you to create your own LCHF recipes.

For your convenience I've added a section with links if you want to read more about LCHF, on page 21. You are also welcome to contact me with any questions.

Dina David
www.lchf-israel.co.il

WHAT IS LCHF? DIET OR LIFESTYLE?

LCHF is the Swedish-English abbreviation of a grass roots movement that started in Sweden at the turn of the century. The abbreviation itself means "low carb high fat" (although some would like to change it to "low carb *healthy* fat"). It is based on the evolution of humankind and our bodies' biochemistry - in short, what our bodies are designed to eat. LCHF has the same basics as the Paleo and Atkin's diets but advocates a more holistic and realistic approach.

What happened? Why Sweden? Here's the story. Just before the beginning of the new millennium, regular people in Sweden, with various health problems, started to read up about evolution, nutrition, and the body's biochemistry and started to put it all together. Until then, they had followed all the health advice presented to them by their physicians and dietitians, in vain. They didn't get healthier; quite the contrary. With the help of the internet, they started researching and educating themselves and soon realized that today's official health advice is based on false research and monetary interests rather than scientific evidence.

Forums started, books were written, and lectures were held, all explaining LCHF. More and more people understood that if they want to be healthy, they had to change the way they thought about food and nutrition and start eating food that the body knows how to handle.

Switching to LCHF has helped many people stabilize their blood sugar levels, blood pressure, and hormonal balance, get better sleep, oral health, and gut health, get rid of acid reflux and heartburn, get rid of joint pain, lose their sugar cravings, and much more, and, as a bonus, they stabilize their weight to its optimal level.

But LCHF is not only a diet. It is about more than what you should or shouldn't eat; it uses a holistic approach and also takes into account ecological aspects. Our health is about more than just the food we eat. LCHF also looks at our health and activity levels, our daily life and stress, our genes, and what we can tolerate. It advocates using locally grown produce and grass-fed meat to help our planet.

Even if you can't afford to buy all organic, as soon as you understand what modern food does to your body and health, and you decide to change your food options to better ones - those that your body is designed to process - you will start to feel the benefits of LCHF. And you won't regret it.

In 2008, LCHF was approved by the Swedish health authorities (*Socialstyrelsen*) as one of the accepted treatments for diabetes and overweight.

In 2013, the Swedish governmental report (*SBU*) concluded, after researching 16,000 studies from all over the world, that: 1) low carbohydrate diets are best for weight loss and blood sugar stability, and 2) there is no evidence that saturated fat causes cardiovascular disease.

WHY SHOULD I EAT LCHF?

About 2.5 million years ago, the first humans started to abandon the rainforests in deepest Africa and walked out onto the savanna. With the change of habitat, a change in human metabolism also began; from formerly eating mostly plants, humans started to hunt. That required a transformation of the human anatomy and digestive biochemistry. Our large intestine regressed, and our enzymes changed to better break down foods from animal sources. That process took hundreds of thousands, if not millions, of years.

Fast forward till today! Modern processed foods have been around for only 100-200 years. Some have been around for even less, maybe only 50 years. But we eat them as if there are no alternatives. What does that do to our bodies? Unfortunately, our digestive system hasn't had time to develop accordingly, and we get sick.

The occurrence of many modern Western diseases, such as cardiovascular disease, diabetes, high blood pressure, cancer, IBS, thyroid problems, and celiac disease, has skyrocketed in recent decades, and, in their wake - an obesity epidemic has erupted. If you ask different experts, they point to different causes, each according to their expertise, whether it is refined sugar, modern wheat, or too much stress. But if you look at the big picture, as in LCHF, you see that they have one thing in common - modern foods.

Our bodies need energy ("fuel") to keep us going and to keep us warm, as well as raw materials ("building blocks") to grow and repair tissues and to fight infections and harmful microbes. Eating according to LCHF gives your body the food for which it was designed.

What's in our food?

We can define and categorize our food in different ways. First, we can consider if a particular food is for energy ("fuel") or for nutrition ("building blocks"), then we can see what type of nutrition (macronutrients and micronutrients) it has. Some foods are good for all purposes; others are good only for one or a few.

The macronutrients are divided into carbohydrates, proteins, and fats, whereas the micronutrients are vitamins and minerals.

What do our bodies use? For fuel, the body can use either sugar or fat. (It can also use protein in certain circumstances but tries to avoid it.) The building blocks come from proteins and fats. Vitamins and minerals are used as the tools for putting the building blocks together.

Proteins are found in both animal and plant-based foods; however, humans digest and absorb the animal proteins better than those from plants. This is due to the different enzymes and other biochemical processes that have developed throughout two million years of evolution. There are even some important nutrients we can get only from animals.

Fats are also found in both animal and plant-based foods. There are different types of fats – saturated, monounsaturated, and polyunsaturated – and we humans need them all. (Yes, the big scare of saturated fats was based on false research and has now finally started to be debunked.)

Carbohydrates, on the other hand, can be found almost only in plant-based foods. (The exception is eggs and dairy products, which count as animal-based foods, and where small amounts of carbohydrates can be found.) Carbohydrate is the general chemical name for what we in everyday life call "sugar," "starch," and "fiber."

Of course, it is not bad per se to eat carbohydrates; the problem occurs when we eat too much and from the wrong sources. The reason for this is the way carbohydrates are digested and how that process impacts our bodies.

Vitamins and **minerals** can be found in both animal and plant-based foods, although in general there are more in animal-based foods. The body's uptake is also easier from animal-based foods.

What do I eat on LCHF? What do I not eat?

In LCHF, there's a generic base that suits more or less everybody; then there are the modifications each person has to make according to their personal needs and lifestyle. Hence, an athlete can eat more carbohydrates on average than a person with diabetes; or a person with sugar addiction might need to avoid some foods that others can eat with no problem. Below are some basic rules. (For more customized options, please consult an LCHF nutritionist.)

You could say that the rule of thumb should be: choose foods with only one ingredient, and avoid anything that has "diet" or "light" printed on the package.

Meat, fish, poultry, and eggs: leave the skin on the chicken and the fat on the meat; use fatty fish like salmon, mackerel, and herring, and don't worry about the amount of eggs you eat. Avoid processed meats, if possible, and choose grass-fed and ecological when available and your budget allows it.

Vegetables: you can eat most vegetables that grow above ground: salad vegetables like tomatoes and cucumbers, of course, but also the cabbage family, and leafy greens. Some non-starchy root vegetables like onions, radishes, kohlrabi, etc. are good options too. Choose local, organically grown produce as much as you can.

Dairy: choose full-fat options: fatty cheeses, and high-fat yoghurts and creams.

Fats: choose the natural ones like butter, coconut oil, tallow, and *schmaltz*. Olive oil is also good if used cold.

Fruits & nuts: most fruits of today contain more water and sugar than anything else, so eat them in moderation and preferably only eat fruit in season. Berries are usually a better choice. Nuts are okay as small snacks but shouldn't be overeaten either, due to their high omega-6 content.

Avoid always: sugar, wheat, margarine (a chemically processed non-food) and any foods that contain these ingredients! Other grains, plant oils (hydrogenated, partly hardened etc.), and artificial sweeteners should also be avoided as much as possible.

Remember that processed foods, even those with "no sugar added" stamped on the package, contain a lot of carbohydrates. Here are some common names you can find for different types of sugar: demerara sugar, brown sugar, muscado sugar, maple syrup, agave, fructose, sacharos, dextrose, corn syrup, HFCS, invert sugar, glucose, glucose syrup, maltodextrin, honey, malt, malt sugar, manitol, sorbitol, molasses, potato starch, rice starch, corn starch, rice syrup, to name just a few. Also remember that artificial sweeteners are equally bad, as the brain perceives them as sugar in all ways and hence reacts as if they were real sugar.

If you are diabetic, pre-diabetic, or overweight, then starches should also be avoided.

Other health issues may require different food options.

Beverages: best is to drink water, but tea and coffee are also okay.

Alcohol: (unless you have a problem with alcohol and need to stay away from it) dry wines and distilled spirits are okay in moderation but can stall weight loss.

Sweets & candy: should be avoided as they mostly contain sugar and artificial coloring; chocolate with high cocoa percentage can be eaten as a treat every now and then.

How much should I eat? When should I eat?

The best rule is to eat when you're hungry and stop when you're not. However, with today's hectic lifestyle, some meals are more time-fixed than others. Two to three full meals a day is optimal. And no, you don't "have to" eat breakfast, nor do you "have to have" two to three snacks in between meals. If you eat enough protein and fat during your meal, it will take you without problems to the next.

As to how much to eat, if your hunger-satiety signals aren't working properly, this could be of help: on your plate, put a protein (preferably from animal source), about the size of your stretched out palm including your fingers, add a nice amount of some fatty sauce, and about a handful of vegetables. If you see that it's not enough to satisfy your hunger, add some more protein and fat.

> ▶ You might not feel the same "stuffed full" feeling as before but a more mild "not hungry" feeling.

LCHF FOR VEGETARIANS

As mentioned previously, our bodies need both fuel and building blocks, and some of these building blocks are found only in animal products. So what does a vegetarian, who wants to eat LCHF, do? Well, if you eat a lacto-ovo-vegetarian diet, there's usually no problem as you will receive the animal proteins from the eggs and the dairy.

However, if you are a vegan, you'll have to carefully monitor your vitamins and minerals and probably need to supplement them. You will, of course, need to eat more carbohydrates than on a normal LCHF diet, so it is important to choose starchy vegetables (e.g. sweet potatoes), over grains. And you should definitely avoid whole grains as they will inhibit mineral and vitamin uptake in the gut. It is also important to soak, sprout, and even ferment and cook legumes and beans, to destroy as much as possible the phytic acid and harmful proteins like lectin.

DO YOU WANT TO KNOW MORE ABOUT LCHF?

This is a cookbook, so I've mentioned only the very basics about LCHF; but you might have a lot of questions, so here are some links to more information. You can also contact me or another LCHF nutritionist for consultation.

www.lchf-israel.co.il/en/

www.dietdoctor.com

www.eatingacademy.com

www.drbriffa.com

www.wheatbellyblog.com

USEFUL KITCHEN TOOLS

Cooking can be quite simple and doesn't need a lot of special tools. Basically, it's enough with a few bowls and pots in different sizes, a sturdy pan, one or two cutting boards, some wooden spoons for stirring, and some good knives. But there is a tool or two that can make cooking both faster and easier, especially if you're constantly in a hurry: the slow cooker and the stick blender.

The **slow cooker** is genius; you put all the ingredients in it in before heading out in the morning, turn it on, and when you get back home in the evening, food's ready. Can it be simpler? And you can even prepare the ingredients the evening before, to save time.

The **stick blender** will help you mush almost anything, thicken soups, and also make instant mayonnaise.

If you have the space in the kitchen and the budget, a food processor can be quite handy if, for example, you want to grind almonds yourself (much cheaper than buying ground almonds).

About the microwave - a good invention, but is it safe? So far I haven't seen any convincing research either way, whether it is harmless or harmful. Do you already have one? Does it help you in your daily life? Then maybe you don't have to throw it out. But if you don't have one, there are other ways to heat a meal, even pretty fast, and you might not need to get one.

INGREDIENTS

Cooking LCHF will require some substitutes for common ingredients, but it really is quite simple. Here are some suggestions:

Sugar and sweeteners

First let me tell you that very quickly after starting LCHF, you'll find that you won't need as much sweet as before. Your taste buds will start to detect the natural subtle sweet flavors in different foods as well as other flavors too. Quite nice!

However, if you want something sweet, like in a cake, you will need to think about what your body can tolerate. Are you diabetic? Avoid glucose. Do you have a sugar addiction? Avoid any sweet at all! Do you have fatty liver problems? Avoid fructose. And so on. In my recipes I have decided to write "sweetener" and, by this, I mean that you have to choose the sweetener that suites your situation. Preferably use a natural sweetener like honey, and try to avoid the artificial ones. The same goes for other recipes you want to convert to LCHF: choose the sweetener that suits your health and goals, and use as little as possible.

▶ Agave syrup may be all natural but it is 100% fructose, and as such, a disaster for your liver. You are better off using honey, date syrup, apple sauce, a mashed banana, etc. as they have a mix of glucose and fructose. Even if you are diabetic!

Remember that the brain believes that any sweet flavor is "sugar" and hence will start the same biochemical processes in your body, regardless of whether you're eating white sugar, raw honey, or an artificial sweetener. This is especially important to consider for diabetics and sugar addicts.

▶ Tip: mixing cinnamon and vanilla gives a mild sweet flavor suitable for cheesecakes or cookies.

Flour and thickeners

All wheat and grains should be avoided because of their harmful proteins. Potato starch doesn't have those but is very high in carbohydrates, so use it sparingly. The best is to use other options; here are a few:

Psyllium husk is the husk of a herb. When it becomes wet, it swells and becomes a soft gel. It can be used for pancakes or to soak up liquids (e.g. in a vegetable casserole dish).

You can use **egg yolks** or **cream** (dairy or coconut) to thicken sauces. To thicken soups, use the stick blender; "blenderize" all or only part of the soup depending on how thick you want it.

Coconut flour is the ground dried fibers left after squeezing out the oil from coconuts. (Note that it's not shredded coconut which is another product, still with its fat content.) The coconut flour is highly absorbent and can be used in breads and cakes. You need very little to substitute for regular flour, maybe one quarter or so.

Nut flours can also be used to stabilize cakes, but they are not absorbent. They are great when making cookies.

For "breading," I sometimes use "**Fibrex**" which is the brand name of a Swedish product - ground dried fibers left from sugar beets after extracting the sugar. I have found the same product under the same name in Israel and hopefully you can find the same or a similar product in a store near you. But don't worry if you don't find it. You can also use shredded coconut or nut flours instead of bread crumbs, or crumbled *grebnitz* (recipe on page 72).

Some simple substitutes for common recipes

Here are some examples on how you can convert regular recipes to LCHF.

British shepherd's pie: use mashed cauliflower (recipe on page 84) instead of mashed potatoes.

Schnitzel: cover the chicken breast or veal with chopped nuts, sesame seeds, ground coconut flakes, or crumbled grebnitz, instead of bread crumbs.

French fries: cut kohlrabi or white radish in sticks and fry.

Spaghetti: cook cabbage or zucchini strips for one minute in slightly salted water and drain.

Some tips and notes about the recipes before you begin

- ▶ Read through the recipe before you begin; preheat the oven and put all the ingredients on the counter for your convenience and to save time.
- ▶ I use a lot of ground almonds. You can buy ready-made almond flour in health food stores, but it is generally cheaper

to make your own at home using a food processor. Peeling the almonds first before grinding is a matter of taste; some prefer the lighter color of blanched almonds, others don't like the texture of the ground skins, and yet others can't be bothered with the peeling. Personally, as I use quite a lot of ground almonds, I decided to peel them only when I make special cakes that need the lighter color.

▶ I always use cream with as high a fat percentage as possible. The same goes for cream cheese and other dairy products, the higher the fat percentage, the better. I try to get butter from grass-fed cows to get a better omega-3/omega-6 balance. Usually, I prefer unsalted butter, so I can add the salt myself according to taste and what I'm making.

▶ Unless otherwise stated, I use size **L** eggs (approximately 60 grams; this differs a bit between countries).

▶ As I grew up in Sweden, I always use the metric system. In cooking, you don't really need to be exact on measurements. Baking, on the other hand, can be a bit trickier, and measurements need to be more exact. However, the larger the batch you're making, the less exact the measurements have to be. (I usually cook and bake by eye, but when writing a cookbook one should be more specific. I'll try!)

▶ For liquids, I use **milliliters (ml)** as I found that "a cup" varies greatly between countries; a US cup = 236 ml, a UK cup = 250 ml, and apparently a Japanese cup = 200 ml! For weights, I use **grams (g)**. I will also use the terms **teaspoon (tsp)** and **tablespoon (tbsp)**. Even though these two measures also vary somewhat between countries (tsp approximately 5 ml, tbsp approximately 15-20 ml), it doesn't really matter as I explained before.

▶ I've stated oven temperatures in both Celsius (**C**) and Fahrenheit (**F**) for your convenience.

1
BREAKFAST

BREAKFAST

First of all, you don't have to eat breakfast. Yes, you heard me right. Not everybody likes or can eat breakfast for various reasons, and that's okay. You shouldn't force yourself to eat when you're not hungry. The reason we've been taught that breakfast is the most important meal, has to do with when our bodies are "sugar driven." Since we haven't eaten while sleeping, our bodies now crave energy to start the day. However, when we've changed to be "fat driven," there's enough energy stored so that we can wait with the day's first meal.

With that said, a lot of people do eat breakfast and then don't feel hungry again until much later and thus eat a combined lunch-supper. (Yes, it is okay to eat only twice a day.)

You can very easily eat any **leftovers** from yesterday's lunch or dinner for breakfast. Or, if you feel that breakfast "should be different," you can make some eggs with or without cheese, meat, fish, or vegetables. Some people think that eating scrambled eggs every day gets boring after a while, but you can vary it with different spices and herbs, or condiments. It won't get more boring than to eat the same cheese sandwich every day with your coffee.

In this chapter, you'll find a few more breakfast ideas.

Porridge

dairy

To save time in the morning, chop the nuts the evening before. You can even make a bunch, mix them with coconut, salt, and cinnamon, and keep the mixture in a tight container in the refrigerator.

You need (1 serving):

a handful of mixed nuts

a dab of butter

1 tbsp coconut flakes

1 egg

50-100 ml full-fat cream

salt to taste

cinnamon, butter, cream (optional)

What to do:

1. Chop the nuts, as coarsely or finely as you wish.
2. Melt the butter in a small pan.
3. Add the chopped nuts, coconut, a few grains of salt, and mix.
4. While stirring, add some of the cream.
5. Add the egg and continue to stir. If needed, add more cream to get the texture you like.

    The porridge is ready when the egg has completely coagulated.

▶ Serve in a bowl with sprinkled cinnamon, a dab of butter, and some cream.

Coconut pancakes

dairy

On weekend mornings everyone by us wakes up and gets up at a different hour and has breakfast whenever it's convenient. I'm usually the first to get up, and by the time the last one's up, I'm ready to have lunch. However, if I want us all to have breakfast together, I've got a trick! I make coconut pancakes and everybody wakes up from the nice smells.

You need:

2 eggs

35 g (approximately 100 ml) dry coconut (to get a smother texture, grind the coconut flakes a little bit more)

100 ml cream

pinch of salt

butter for frying

1-2 tsp psyllium husk (optional) - to get a thicker batter (Swedish pancakes are thin whereas American pancakes are thick.)

What to do:

1. Mix all ingredients in a bowl and let stand for 5-7 minutes.
2. Melt some butter in a pan on medium heat.
3. Spoon batter into the pan and fry the pancakes on both sides.

▶ Serve with cinnamon, cottage cheese, or berries. (The cinnamon can be added to the batter, and the berries can be slightly pureed to make a sauce.)

Egg milk latte

dairy, parve

This is a good, quite quick and filling, breakfast option if you don't like eating breakfast or are in a hurry. The egg milk is actually not milk at all. And you can even make it 100% parve.

It is also suitable as parve whitener in your coffee or if you want your latte to be dairy free.

Try it with different flavors, or use it in your coffee or tea instead of milk or cream.

There are a few recipes, here is a basic one.

You get the best results with a stick blender.

You need:

25 g butter (unsalted) or coconut fat

1 egg yolk

½ tsp vanilla

150-200 ml hot water

Here are some suggested flavorings:

1 tsp instant coffee powder

1 tsp cocoa powder

½ tsp ground cinnamon

½ tsp ground cardamom

What to do:

1. Melt the butter or coconut fat in a pot, a bowl with high sides, or a tall glass.
2. Add a flavoring you like and mix a little.
3. Add the egg yolk and mix well.
4. While mixing, pour in the hot water and continue to mix some more, so on one hand foam is created and on the other hand the egg won't solidify.

Drink!

▶ You can keep the egg milk refrigerated for quite a few days. (Mix it a little before use.)

▶ Experiment and try with more or less water, flavors, etc. to get your favorite beverage.

Shakshouka

dairy, parve, meat (depending on the frying fat and extra ingredients)

Shakshouka is a traditional Israeli egg dish (thought to be Tunisian in origin) eaten for breakfast, brunch, or supper. Apart from eggs, the most important ingredient is tomatoes. There are those who would say you have to use fresh tomatoes, and there are those who think crushed canned ones are good enough. Then there's the question of what to add to the tomatoes. There are those who won't add anything or only some onions and a little bit of salt, and there are those who will add any vegetable lying around.

My husband is of the latter sort and here's a version he frequently makes. All quantities are approximate as that's the way he cooks, but don't be afraid to experiment yourself! And play with different types of herbs and spices, chopped olives, mushrooms and so on to find your favorite Shakshouka.

You need:

1–1.5 kg soft tomatoes or the equivalent in canned tomatoes

1–2 big onions

2–3 bell peppers of different colors

4–6 garlic cloves

a few drops of Tabasco

salt to taste

1–2 eggs per person

some fat for frying

What to do:

1. Peel and chop the onions and the garlic.
2. Wash and cut the peppers in short strips or small squares.
3. If you use fresh tomatoes, wash them and cut them into smaller cubes. (If you want, you can skin them first, but it's not necessary.) If you use canned tomatoes, just open the cans.
4. Melt the fat in a skillet and sauté the onions, garlic, and peppers.
5. Add tomatoes and seasoning, and cook at low temperature to a thick sauce, while stirring every now and then.
6. Crack the eggs onto the sauce and let them cook on top of the sauce, at low temperature, until they are as done as you like them. You can put a lid on to make the white stiffen quicker.

▶ You can sprinkle some feta cheese on top before serving or add small sausages to cook in the sauce.

2
LUNCH/DINNER

LUNCH/DINNER

There isn't a big difference between lunch and dinner in LCHF; the easiest way to make lunch is to have leftovers from yesterday's dinner, so make it a habit to always make more than you will eat at one meal. By the way, it is always a good idea to make extra and freeze to have on the go or for those days when you don't have time to cook.

You can probably use most of your regular meat and fish recipes and only substitute flour and such, but to get you going, I've collected a few easy samples of good lunches and dinners in this chapter.

Cheese & herb pie

dairy

An especially cheesy cheese pie for a dairy meal. Make the crust with some chopped walnuts for texture and flavor.

You need:

300 g mixed hard cheeses (Kashkaval, Cheddar, etc.)

225 g cream cheese

1 tsp dry oregano or other herb

250 ml full-fat cream

4 eggs

salt and pepper to taste

sliced tomato for garnish (optional)

What to do:

1. Preheat the oven to 175° C/345° F.
2. Make the savory pie crust on page 133 and prebake it.
3. Grate the cheese and mix all ingredients together.
4. Pour the batter into the prebaked crust and put the tomato slices on top.
5. Bake the pie for about 40 minutes until set or golden brown.

Cheese and tuna casserole dish

dairy

Do you know how to cook nail soup? This may not be a soup recipe but nevertheless that's how I felt when my sister, one Shavuot morning, suddenly announced that I was in charge of lunch for all of us (her family and mine). She announced and I started to look through cupboards and the refrigerator to get some inspiration. This casserole dish may be made "on a nail," but everyone licked their fingers.

You need:

200-250 g tuna in water

1 red bell pepper

75 g hard cheese (flavorful)

250 g cottage cheese

5 eggs

dill to taste

salt and pepper to taste

What to do:

1. Preheat the oven to 175° C / 345° F.
2. Chop the bell pepper and the dill, grate the cheese, and drain the tuna.
3. Mix all ingredients in a bowl, and add salt and pepper to taste.
4. Pour the mixture into a casserole dish and bake for 30-40 minutes or until golden brown.

▶ You can save some of the grated cheese and sprinkle on top of the casserole dish before baking.

▶ Instead of a big casserole dish, pour the mixture into muffin forms and bake. This way you can freeze the ready "food-muffins" and have them any day on-the-go.

Chicken drumsticks in curry

meat

Making festive dinners on a weekday can be very easy; you don't need a lot of ingredients, and letting it cook in the oven frees time for other things.

You need (3-4 servings):

8-10 chicken drumsticks

300-400 ml coconut cream

2 tbsp curry powder

3-4 cm fresh ginger (optional)

salt to taste

What to do:

1. Preheat the oven to 200° C/390° F.
2. Place the drumsticks in a baking dish.
3. Mix the coconut cream with the curry powder and some salt. (Add grated fresh ginger if you like.)
4. Pour it all on top of the chicken and place in the oven.
5. Bake for 45-60 minutes or until the chicken is ready.

▶ Serve the chicken with cauliflower "rice" (see recipe page 74) and pour some of the curry sauce on top.

47 | Lunch/Dinner

Stuffed chicken

meat

One time I got a whole chicken that was quite large and it reminded me that stuffed chicken was something I hadn't done for a very long time. Considering that most stuffing is bread or rice based, that's not surprising. Nor would you probably want to stuff a chicken for a quick mid-week dinner. But for Shabbat, why not? And you know what? The same stuffing could go into a turkey for Thanksgiving.

So what kind of stuffing do you do for LCHF? I looked in the refrigerator to see what would inspire me and came up with this mixture.

You need:

1 large chicken

½ cabbage

2 medium onions

½ red pepper

½ yellow pepper

½ cup walnuts

fresh dill to taste

salt, pepper, garlic powder, and sweet paprika to taste

1 grated sour apple (optional)

What to do:

1. Preheat the oven to 185° C/365° F.
2. Cut half of the cabbage and one of the onions in strips and spread them in a baking pan large enough to hold the chicken.
3. Chop the rest of the cabbage and put in a mixing bowl.
4. Chop the other onion, the peppers, and the dill finely and the walnuts coarsely. Grate the apple if using. Add all to the bowl as well as the seasonings and mix.
5. Stuff the chicken and then season it all around with the same spices as in the stuffing. Put the chicken in the pan.
6. Bake for almost an hour, until the chicken is done.

▶ Serve with a lemon-mayo sauce (see recipe page 86).

▶ If you have leftover stuffing from filling the chicken, mix it with an egg and bake it in a casserole dish.

Chuck in wine

meat

Ever since my American husband introduced me to the slow cooker, I've used it very often. (I had never heard of a slow cooker or crock pot until then.) What a help when life gets hectic! And what a pity I didn't know about it when the kids were small.

Here is a very simple basic recipe of chuck in wine. Apart from being very easy to prepare, there are two more pluses for the busy person:

- ▶ This meat dish is quite cheap, especially if you buy the meat when you find it on sale and put it in the freezer until needed.
- ▶ Cut up any leftovers in slices and freeze. Then you just thaw as much as you need for a meal.

You need:

1–2 kg boneless chuck, such as shoulder, boneless breast etc.

2–3 large onions

1–2 bay leaves

1–2 glasses red wine

salt and pepper to taste

What to do:

1. Chop the onions and put them in the slow cooker.
2. Add the meat and the bay leaves.
3. Pour the wine over.
4. Salt and pepper the meat.
5. Turn the slow cooker on low for 6–10 hours or high for 4–8 hours. (It depends on the amount of meat, but don't worry, it can hardly be overcooked.)

- ▶ If your meat is frozen, it can either be defrosted overnight in the refrigerator or put in the slow cooker still frozen, depending on how much time you have.
- ▶ You can, of course, change the wine to broth and experiment with other spices.

"Almost goulash" stew

meat

The first time I had goulash here in Israel it was made with tomatoes, and I was surprised as, according to what I've learned, a real goulash isn't made with tomatoes at all but with red peppers. I've made goulash both ways since, but I call the one with tomatoes "almost goulash." This stew gets very rich, with a hearty taste, as most of the liquids come from the meat itself.

You need:

2 kg goulash meat, cut in big cubes

2-3 onions

5-6 garlic cloves

200 g tomato paste

1-2 bay leaves

5-6 black pepper corns, crushed

100 ml dry red wine

schmaltz or tallow for frying

What to do:

1. Put some fat in a slow cooker and turn it on.
2. While the fat is heating up a little, cut the onions in strips or chunks, and mash the garlic cloves a bit.
3. Add them to the slow cooker and stir a little.
4. Add the meat cubes in and stir occasionally to sear them a little all around.
5. Add the crushed pepper corns and the bay leaves.
6. Mix the tomato paste with the wine and pour over the meat.
7. Put the lid on the slow cooker and let the meat cook (stirring occasionally) until it's tender and starts to fall apart - 4 to 10 hours, depending on your slow cooker.

▶ Serve with some mashed cauliflower (to soak up the sauce!) and a green salad.

Roast in pesto

meat

I always liked cooking with my kids. That was true when they were small, and it still is, although they've reached their 20s. Trying new culinary ideas can render many laughs.
Following is a roast variation my son and I invented.

You need (4-6 servings):

1 kg boneless ribs or similar

1 bunch cilantro

½ bunch parsley

6 cloves garlic

½ medium onion

½ cup olive oil

2 tbsp lemon or lime juice

40 g pine nuts

pinch of salt

if you like it a bit spicier, add a piece of hot red pepper

What to do:

1. Preheat the oven to 250° C/ 480° F.
2. Put the meat in a baking pan.
3. Toast the pine nuts slightly.
4. Put them, the leaves and the other ingredients in a blender and mix to a spreadable texture.
5. Spread about half on top of the meat and put in the oven.
6. Bake for 10-15 minutes.
7. Take the pan out of the oven and lower the temperature to 180° C / 355° F.
8. Turn the roast and spread the rest of the pesto on it.
9. Bake for another 30-45 minutes, depending on how rare or done you want the roast.
10. Take the roast out of the oven and let it rest for about 10 minutes before cutting it in thin slices.

▶ Serve with a crisp green salad or make a nice cauliflower "rice" to go with it (see recipe page 74).

Minced meat in 3 different ways, at least

meat

Minced, or ground, meat can be the base for many quick and tasty dishes. The all-time, easiest way to prepare minced meat is to season it with some salt, pepper, and garlic powder and then fry patties/hamburgers. But you can also make other dishes that are just as simple, with only a few more ingredients.

The best minced meat is the one you get ground fresh at the butcher. Make sure the fat content is at least around 20%. You can also ask the butcher to grind the meat twice to get a finer texture.

Here are three basic recipes: for burgers, meatloaf, and meat sauce. All can be varied in numerous ways, and I have added some suggestions for you.

1. Burgers

You need:

200-250 g minced meat per person

salt, pepper, and garlic powder to taste

some schmaltz, tallow, or coconut fat for frying

Add one or more of the following (per 200-250 g meat):

1 tbsp chopped fresh onions

1 tbsp chopped sautéed onions

1 tsp unsweetened mustard

1 tsp tomato paste

1 tsp dried herbs such as basil, oregano, or marjoram

1 tbsp chopped fresh herbs such as parsley or cilantro

a pinch of different spices such as ground mustard seeds, sweet paprika, hot paprika, or cardamom

What to do:

1. Mix all the ingredients in a bowl.
2. Form burgers and fry in a hot pan to desired doneness.

▶ Serve with some lettuce, tomato slices, pickles, onion rings and mayo, just like a "regular" burger. You can also add some kohlrabi fries (recipe on page 25) and you'll get the best "happy meal" ever.

▶ And while you're already at it, make a few extra burgers but don't fry them yet. Wrap each patty in baking paper or plastic film and pack them in an airtight container. Freeze and you have ready burgers for another day. (You don't need to thaw them more than a few minutes before frying them.)

2. Meatloaf

You need:

1 kg minced meat

2 eggs

salt, pepper, and garlic powder to taste

Add one or more of the following:

a small chopped raw or sautéed onion

sautéed mushroom pieces

chopped pickles

1-2 tbsp toasted pine nuts or sunflower seeds

2 tbsp unsweetened mustard

2 tbsp tomato paste

2 tbsp chopped fresh herbs such as parsley or cilantro

2 tsp dried herbs such as basil, oregano, or marjoram

a pinch of different spices such as ground mustard seeds, sweet paprika, hot paprika, or cardamom

What to do:

1. Preheat the oven to 175° C/345° F.
2. Mix all the ingredients in a bowl.
3. Divide the meat mixture in two loaf pans. There's no need to grease them.
4. Place the pans in the oven and bake for 45-50 minutes.

▶ If you want to make a "fancier" meatloaf, instead of mixing in the sautéed mushrooms or pickles, place the meat in the loaf pan and make a long groove in it. Place the mushrooms/pickles, or maybe some whole peeled hardboiled eggs, in the groove. Cover up with the meat and bake as in the recipe.

▶ You can grease the pan if you like and sprinkle the pan sides with some sesame seeds or chopped nuts.

3. Meat sauce

You need:

200–250 g minced meat per person

½ medium onion

salt, pepper, and garlic powder to taste

some schmaltz, tallow, or coconut fat for frying

(100–150 ml water)

Add one or more of the following (per 200–250 g meat):

1 chopped tomato

½ tbsp tomato paste

1 tsp dried herbs such as basil, oregano, or marjoram

1 tbsp chopped fresh herbs such as parsley or cilantro

a pinch of different spices such as ground sweet paprika, hot paprika, or cardamom

100 ml coconut cream

50 ml red dry wine

What to do:

1. Slice or chop the onion and fry in some fat.
2. Add the minced meat and fry it while stirring occasionally until all is cooked through. (You'll see the meat changing color when it's done.)
3. Add the seasoning and any of the suggested alternatives.
4. Add some water if you don't use coconut cream or wine, and let simmer for a few minutes.

▶ Serve on top of some grated and sautéed cabbage (recipe on page 62), mashed cauliflower (recipe on page 84), or cauliflower rice (recipe on page 74).

▶ Here too, make some extra sauce and freeze in portion containers for another time.

▶ By the way, you can also make the sauce in a pot; add some more liquid and some cabbage, carrots, or other vegetable, to make a hearty meat-vegetable soup for cold days.

Swedish cabbage pudding

meat

Despite the name, this dish is actually more meat than cabbage and more casserole dish than pudding. Nevertheless, it is a good all-in-one-pot meal that can be made in large quantity and frozen in pieces for future use.

At the end, I've added a "quick fix" for the really lazy among us.

You need:

500 g minced meat

1 onion

1 egg

½ cabbage

salt, pepper, and other herbs and spices according to taste

some schmaltz, tallow, or coconut fat for frying

What to do:

1. Preheat the oven to 175° C/345° F.
2. Cut the cabbage in pieces or 1-2 cm wide strips and sauté a little. Set aside.
3. Chop the onion and sauté a little.
4. Add the minced meat and fry it while stirring occasionally until all is cooked through. (You'll see the meat changing color when it's done.)
5. Let the fried meat cool a little and then add eggs and spices. Mix well.
6. In a casserole dish, put a layer of cabbage, then a layer of meat sauce. Repeat twice and end with a layer of cabbage on top.
7. Bake the pudding for 45-60 minutes.

▶ Quick fix for the really "lazy": Mix the sautéed cabbage with the meat sauce. Pour all into the casserole dish and bake as above.

Simplest salmon ever

dairy

And it gets even simpler if you have an electric pan that's big enough!

You need:

salmon filet - 150-200 g fish per person

some cream

a bunch of fresh dill

tomato slices

onion slices

salt and pepper to taste

butter for the pan

What to do:

1. Preheat the oven to 175° C/345° F and grease a baking pan with some butter.
2. Put the salmon filets in the pan.
3. Season with salt and pepper.
4. Put the tomato and onion slices on the filets as well as some sprigs of dill.
5. Pour cream over all of it.
6. Bake for about 20 minutes or until the fish is done.

▶ You can also do the dish with salmon steaks or any other fish filet you like.

Tuna patties

dairy, parve, meat (depending on the frying fat)

Something quick for those days you don't know what to cook.
And while you're at it, make a bunch and freeze! They are great to just pull out and have on the go, or to bring to a 10-hour day at the university.

You need:

100-125 g tuna in water

1 egg

dill, onion, and red pepper, according to taste and imagination

salt and pepper to taste

some fat for frying

What to do:

1. Drain the tuna and chop the dill, onion and red pepper.
2. Mix all ingredients in a bowl.
3. Form palm-sized patties and fry in a pan on both sides.

▶ Serve with some mayo or other creamy sauce and some vegetables.

Upside-down pizza

dairy

I got this recipe from my niece, a young student, who makes this easy pizza when she wants a quick satisfying dinner. It's a great way to use up all those cheese ends that tend to accumulate in the fridge.

You need:

500 g assorted hard cheeses

3 tbsp mayonnaise

4 eggs

150 g tomato paste

salt, pepper, and dry oregano to taste

Toppings such as:

olives, anchovies, peppers, capers, feta cheese, onions, fresh basil, etc.

What to do:

1. Preheat the oven to 225° C/435° F and put baking paper on a cookie sheet or in a pizza pan.
2. Grate the cheese and put in a bowl.
3. Add the mayo and the eggs and mix well.
4. Spread the cheese mixture on the baking paper (approximately 1 cm thick) and put in the oven.
5. Bake for 10 minutes until the cheese starts to turn golden.
6. Take it out and let it cool for a minute.
7. In the meantime, mix the tomato paste with the salt, pepper, and oregano.
8. Spread it on the cheese crust and then add your topping.
9. Bake for another 10-15 minutes.

    Let the pizza cool for a few minutes before slicing it.

▶ Serve with coleslaw or another nice salad.

3

SIDE DISHES

SIDE DISHES

This is where most people have trouble cooking LCHF; what should they use instead of potatoes, rice, and pasta? It is actually quite simple as there are so many more vegetables than just lettuce and cucumber. What about mashed cauliflower instead of mashed potatoes, or sautéed cabbage instead of pasta? In this chapter, you will find those recipes as well as a bunch more ideas.

Schmaltz and grebnitz

meat

If you didn't see how your grandmother made schmaltz…
You use the same technique to make tallow from beef fat, but then cut the fat pieces in smaller cubes before starting to melt them, otherwise they'll get a crisp crust while there's still a lot of fat inside the pieces. (This is very tasty to snack but it will render less tallow.)

You need:

As much chicken fat and skin trimmings as possible

What to do:

1. Clean the skin from leftover feathers and, if necessary, cut it into smaller pieces.
2. Put all in a wide pan and heat at low temperature.
3. Let it melt until all the skin is golden and crispy. (Stir occasionally.)
4. Pour the melted fat into jars and let cool.

▶ Use the schmaltz when you want to sauté onions for meat dishes, or just to fry meat.

▶ Use the fried skin, grebnitz, as snacks or crumble to use as flavored crumbs.

A stewed side dish

dairy, parve, meat (depending on the frying fat and type of cream)

Well, actually this is going to be a few recipes in one, as you can use the same method for different vegetables.

You need:

1 head of cabbage or cauliflower, or a bag of fresh spinach

1 medium onion

a nice dab of butter, coconut fat, or schmaltz

100-200 ml full-fat dairy cream or coconut cream

salt and pepper to taste

a bunch of parsley or cilantro (optional)

What to do:

1. Clean the vegetable and then either slice the cabbage, break the cauliflower in small flowerets, or chop the spinach, depending on what vegetable you chose.
2. Slice or chop the onion.
3. Melt the fat in a big pot.
4. Add the onions and sauté them a little.
5. Add the chopped vegetable, cream, and seasonings.
6. Cover the pot and simmer at very low heat until the vegetable is soft.
7. Chop some fresh parsley or cilantro and sprinkle on top before serving.

Cauliflower rice

dairy, parve, meat (depending on the frying fat)

This "rice" can also be made by cooking the grated cauliflower for a few minutes in salted water, but I like it better sautéed. Then I can sauté chopped onions with it too.

You need:

1 cauliflower

a nice dab of butter, coconut fat, or schmaltz

salt to taste

chopped onion according to taste

What to do:

1. Grate the cauliflower.
2. Melt the fat in a pot and add the cauliflower. Add onion if using.
3. Add some salt and let it sauté slowly, while stirring occasionally, for about 10 minutes.

Egg noodles

parve

One of the frequent "problems" encountered when starting LCHF is to know what to substitute for common food items used before.
Friday night. Shabbat dinner with the traditional family dishes: chicken soup with noodles! How do you do that on LCHF? Well, there's the "Chinese way" of stirring in beaten eggs to make egg drop soup (think Chinese corn soup), but what if you want the more substantial noodle texture? Even that can be done in LCHF.

You need:

4 eggs

2 tsp psyllium husk

a bunch of parsley

a pinch of salt

garlic powder, ground mustard seeds, hot pepper, etc. (optional)

What to do:

1. Preheat the oven to 150°C/300°F and line a cookie sheet with baking paper.
2. Chop the parsley and mix all the ingredients very well.
3. Let sit for about 5-7 minutes and then spread it evenly on the baking paper. It should be a thin layer, only 3-4 mm thick.
4. Bake for about 10 minutes, just until the batter stiffens and starts to be very light golden.
5. Take the pan out of the oven and quickly roll up the baked batter together with the paper.

    Let cool.

▶ 6. Unroll and remove the baking paper. Then carefully roll it up again and slice thinly.

▶ Serve the noodles still rolled in the soup.

▶ You can create different types of noodles by cutting the slices thinner or thicker ("spaghetti," "fettuccini," or "linguini"), or by cutting the rolls lengthwise first to make flakes ("filini" or "quadretti"), and then serve them with a sauce or as a side dish as you would any noodle. Wide strips can even be used to make lasagna.

▶ Depending on the type of baking paper you use, you might need to very, very slightly grease the paper before baking the noodles, to make it easier to peel.

Green beans in tomato sauce

parve

This is a recipe I learned from my sister many years ago when she had a bunch of small kids and was always cooking in the fastest and simplest way possible. It's so simple it doesn't really need a recipe, but I'm adding it here as it's such a good companion to almost everything - meat, poultry, fish, hardboiled eggs - you name it! You can also make a large batch and then freeze it in smaller portions, ready to heat and eat. And one more thing - some people might get their sweet tooth triggered by the tomato flavor. No problem! It's tasty without the tomato paste too.

You need:

50 g coconut oil

1 medium-large onion

4 cloves garlic

frozen green beans

100 g tomato paste

1-2 glasses of water

salt and pepper to taste

What to do:

1. Chop or slice the onions and peel the garlic.
2. Heat the oil in a big pot.
3. Add the onions and sauté them till they're soft but not brown.
4. Crush the garlic and add it too. Stir a little.
5. Add the frozen beans (no need to thaw them first), the tomato paste, salt and pepper to taste, and some of the water. Stir a little.
6. Cover and let simmer at low heat, stirring occasionally.

   It's ready when the beans are completely thawed and warm but not over cooked.

Herb butter

dairy

Herb butter is a perfect addition to any fish or vegetable dish. And it's very easy to make your own! Why not make a larger batch and keep in the freezer?

You need:

butter

salt to taste

one or more of the following:

finely chopped fresh garlic, chives, or onion of different sorts

tomato paste

finely chopped herbs such as parsley, cilantro, dill, or basil

ground dried spices such as za'atar (hyssop, marjoram), garlic powder, black pepper, hot pepper, lemon pepper, or onion powder

What to do:

1. Put the butter in a mixing bowl.
2. Add your seasoning. Let your imagination and taste buds guide you.
3. Add some salt and mix it all together until more or less homogenous.
4. Spread a baking sheet on the counter and put the butter mixture on top, then wrap the butter with the baking sheet and start to roll it while pressing a little, to make a long "sausage," 3-4 cm in diameter.
5. Wrap the baking sheet more tightly and put the roll in the freezer.

▶ Cut off a slice whenever you need some flavored butter.

Mashed cauliflower

dairy (parve)

One of the top favorites of the whole family! (Never any leftovers.) This is the novice version, but I've added some extra ingredients for those who want them.
You can, of course, make the mash parve too; see further down.

You need:

1 big cauliflower

250 ml full-fat cream

50 g butter

salt to taste

What to do:

1. Clean the cauliflower and break it into smaller pieces.
2. Put them in a pot and add the cream.
3. Let steam on low heat until the cauliflower is soft. Stir occasionally so the cauliflower will be cooked evenly.
4. Mash the cauliflower with the cream.
5. Add butter and salt and mix.

▶ For parve: just steam the cauliflower in a small amount of water that you pour out before mixing the mash with 2-3 tbsp coconut or olive oil instead.

▶ For more "advanced" versions do one or more of the following: chop and sauté an onion in the pot before adding the cauliflower and cream, chop some parsley or other herb and add it to the mash, season the mash with ground garlic, black pepper, or other spices.

Quick mayo

parve

First, I got tired of buying ready-made mayonnaise with a long list of undesired ingredients. Then, Hubby got tired of trying to "pour the oil in a thin steady stream" and have the mayo still separate. After some online research and some experimenting in the kitchen, we found this fool-proof way of doing the most delicious, creamy, home-made mayonnaise I've ever tasted. And it never separates! (As long as you leave the salt till the very end.)

You need:

2 egg yolks

1-2 tbsp lemon juice

½ tsp ground mustard seeds

250 ml cold pressed oil (mild olive/non-GMO canola or palm)

pinch of salt - only at the end!

other seasoning such as garlic, dill, more lemon, black pepper

What to do:

You need a stick blender and a high narrow jar. (The jar that comes with many stick blenders is perfect.)

1. Put the egg yolks at the bottom of the jar.
2. Add lemon juice, mustard seeds, and other seasoning. (But not yet the salt!)
3. Pour the oil over.
4. Put the stick blender all the way down and start it. Hold it there for a little while and then, very slowly, start to lift it upwards. You can see the mayo thicken as you pull!
5. Add the salt and mix. (You can add a few drops of water if you think the mayo is too thick.)
6. Transfer the mayonnaise to a container with a tight lid. Keep in the refrigerator.

▶ Here are some nice variations: **Swedish Béarnaise sauce** - add ground tarragon, chopped shallot, a few drops of white wine vinegar. **Swedish Remoulade sauce** - add chopped pickles, capers, and parsley or chives.

87 | Side Dishes

Salads

parve

LCHF doesn't mean "no" carbs, so we can eat vegetables too. But what types and how much? Well, that depends on how much carbohydrate you want to consume; some people can eat more, and some can only use vegetables as "garnish."

When you want to go low on your carbs, it's even more important that the vegetables you do eat are as nutritious as possible. Most people think of salad as a leaf of lettuce and maybe a slice of tomato, but it can be so much more!

Here are two colorful, easy salads that take no time to prepare.

89 | Side Dishes

1. Spinach salad

You need:

a bunch of spinach leaves

1 orange

¼ – ½ red onion (depends on how much you like onion)

½ cup roasted hazelnuts

What to do:

1. Clean the spinach and chop it a little. Place the chopped spinach in a bowl.

2. Peel the orange and cut each wedge into 3-4 pieces. Add to the bowl. (You can squeeze some of the pieces a little for juice.)

3. Cut the onion in very thin slices and add to the bowl. Mix it all.

4. Chop the hazelnuts coarsely and sprinkle them on top.

2. Cabbage & root salad

You need:

¼ cabbage

¼ cauliflower

1-2 carrots

½ - 1 red beet

lemon juice

olive oil

salt and pepper to taste

What to do:

1. Clean and chop the cabbage and the cauliflower in small pieces.
2. Peel the carrots and the beet and grate them coarsely.
3. Put everything in a bowl and mix.
4. Season with lemon juice, olive oil, salt, and pepper.

Onion casserole dish

parve

Great as a side dish to any meal and can be frozen as well.
As with most of my recipes, I also play around with this one - sometimes I use only raw onions, and sometimes I sauté part of them; sometimes I use marjoram, and sometimes I use other herbs.

You need:

3 large onions

2 tbsp dry marjoram

6 eggs

2 tbsp psyllium husk

salt and pepper to taste

sesame seeds (optional)

What to do:

1. Preheat the oven to 175° C / 345° F and grease a casserole dish. You can sprinkle some sesame seeds in the pan if you want.
2. Mix the eggs with the psyllium husk and let sit for 5 to 7 minutes.
3. Chop the onions and mix them with the eggs and other ingredients.
4. Pour into the casserole dish. Sprinkle some sesame seeds on top if using.
5. Bake for 40 minutes or until the casserole dish is set and nice golden brown.

4
SNACKS

SNACKS

When eating LCHF, you will notice that you don't need to snack as much as before. When your body is sugar driven, it's very easy to get into sugar dips, and the best way to get out of them is to eat something. The same goes for sugar addiction; your body wants to continue feeding it. But when you are fat driven, there are no sugar dips, and the sweet tooth mellows. Nevertheless, sometimes you might want a snack when it's still a few hours until the next meal; so what can you have?

A simple snack can be a few nuts or olives, or maybe a piece of cheese. In this chapter, I've gathered some ideas for snacks that are more than just that. Some snacks are also good to have "on the go" or at the buffet table as finger food.

A word of caution - if you notice that you want to snack a little too much or a little too often, maybe you are actually hungry and should eat something more substantial.

Eggs

dairy, parve, meat

Eggs are one of the best foods there is; you can prepare them in so many ways, eat them for any type of meal, and even snack on them. The variations are numerous, ranging from regular boiled to more fancy "Eggs Benedict." Actually, "Deviled Eggs" can be the nicest party food! An egg is also nature's own vitamin pill; "A few eggs a day will keep the doctor away!"

My day isn't 100% if I don't start it with two scrambled eggs in butter and salt. And there are always hard-boiled eggs in our fridge.

And remember, contrary to what's been hammered into our heads, you almost can't have too many eggs. The only downside with too many is that you might get tired of them!

Variations for your morning omelet

Add to your regular plain omelet one or more of the following: chopped herbs, sautéed onions, cheese cubes, pastrami or sausage pieces (then of course use coconut fat or schmaltz instead of butter), different spices, yesterday's left-overs, tuna, sardines in tomato sauce, etc.

Variations for hard boiled eggs - deviled eggs

1. Mix mayo/butter/crème fraiche/sour cream with one or more of the following: chopped herbs, fish eggs, curry powder, pickles, grated flavorful cheese, or small pieces of fried pastrami or sausage.
2. Cut the hard-boiled eggs in half and scoop out the yolks.
3. Mix the yolks with the filling and put it back into the eggs.

Variations for egg salad

1. Boil some eggs.
2. Peel and mash them and mix with mayo/butter/crème fraiche/sour cream.
3. Season with salt, pepper, and a dash of sweet paprika, or any of the suggestions above for hard-boiled eggs.

Cheeses

dairy

Cheese is good for those who can tolerate it. It's true that cheese and yoghurts have only been around since domestication of animals, some 20,000 years ago, and hence followers of the Paleolithic diet tend to cut it out of their regime. However, in LCHF we also look at what the body can tolerate, and as there are human populations who have developed enzymes that break down lactose and milk proteins, you can have dairy products if your body accepts them.

- ▶ Choose full-fat cheeses over low-fat.
- ▶ The more aged a cheese, the lower the lactose content.

1. Tzaziki-like cheese dip

Quantities needed for this dip really depend on how solid or soft you like the dip to be. The same goes for how much garlic and herbs you want to add.

You need:

cream cheese

sour cream

garlic cloves

fresh dill or mint leaves

salt and pepper to taste

cucumber (optional)

What to do:

1. Mix the cream cheese and the sour cream.
2. Press the garlic and chop the herb of choice.
3. Add them to the dip together with the salt and pepper, and mix.

▶ You can also add some finely chopped cucumber to the dip.

2. Blue cheese balls

Quantities needed depend on how solid or soft your blue cheese is.

You need:

a piece of blue cheese

cream cheese

onion (optional)

walnuts (optional)

What to do:

1. Grate the blue cheese and mix it with the cream cheese.
2. Form small balls with your hands.

▶ You can role the balls in finely chopped onions or walnuts, or decorate with a piece of whole walnut on top of the ball.

5
DESSERTS & CANDY

DESSERTS & CANDY

A funny thing happened in my family when we started to eat LCHF; we stopped making desserts. It was as if we totally forgot there was such a thing. Food was enough, plenty and delicious. The first time I noticed this happening was a Friday evening when we had guests. Suddenly I realized that I had forgotten to prepare something - the dessert. I quickly put out a platter of fruit, a bowl of chocolate pieces, and some nuts, and voila the "problem" was solved. Since then, I have made LCHF-desserts and even some "candy" to have at special occasions.

You'll find some suggestions here.

Ice cream

dairy, parve

Homemade ice cream is very easy to make. And tastier! You don't even need an ice cream machine.

The easiest is to just whip some cream, add a flavor, and then freeze it. However here is a recipe that also uses egg yolks, and a few suggestions for interesting flavors.

This recipe can be made dairy or parve, depending on the type of cream you use.

You need:

200 ml whipping cream (non-sweetened) or coconut cream

1 tsp vanilla extract

2 egg yolks

Add one or more of the following (adjust quantities according to taste):

1 tbsp unsweetened cocoa powder

50 g grated dark chocolate

150 g semi-mashed berries

3 tbsp toasted chopped nuts and/or coconut flakes

1 tsp ground cinnamon

1 tsp instant coffee powder

2 tbsp bourbon, whiskey, or flavored liquor (pay attention to the sugar content!)

a few drops of mint extract

For the courageous, add a few drops of Tabasco (wonderful with vanilla ice cream!) or crushed hot pepper flakes (for chocolate ice cream)

▶ **What to do:**

1. Mix the egg yolks with the flavoring and whip them fluffy.

2. Whip the cream and fold it gently into the egg mixture.

3. Pour into a container and freeze until set.

▶ If you use coconut cream, it might not get as fluffy as dairy cream. You can then whip one of the egg whites and add to the mixture before freezing.

▶ The ice cream gets a bit harder than bought ice cream due to the lower sugar content, so just remember to take it out of the freezer 10-15 minutes before serving.

Coconut pudding with apple sauce

parve

This dairy-free pudding can be eaten as a dessert or as a light meal when you're not that hungry. Of course, some of the coconut cream can be changed for dairy cream if you prefer.

For a water bath, you need two oven pans: one for the pudding and one slightly bigger. Pour water into the bigger pan, up to about half the height of the smaller one. This way of baking heats the pudding more evenly throughout, without making a hard crust.

You need:

3 eggs

100 g (approximately 300 ml) coconut flakes

1-2 tbsp sweetener

100 ml coconut cream

a few apples

toasted hazelnuts (optional)

What to do:

1. Preheat the oven to 160° C/320° F and prepare the water bath.
2. Put the eggs, coconut flakes, sweetener, and coconut cream in a bowl, mix well, and then pour the batter into the smaller pan.
3. Place it in the water bath, and then put the whole thing in the oven. Bake for 35-40 minutes, until set and the pudding just starts to be golden.
4. In the meantime, peel and core the apples. Cut them in smaller cubes.
5. Place the apples in a pot over low heat. Let them cook down to sauce, stirring occasionally.
▶ Serve the pudding lukewarm with the applesauce. You can also chop some toasted hazelnuts and sprinkle on top.

113 | Desserts & Candy

Chocolate fun

dairy, parve

Today, it's quite easy to get a hold of chocolate with a high cocoa content; there are many companies that make ready-to-buy chocolate bars with 70, 85, and even 90% cocoa mass in them. Although, most often, these chocolate bars also contain some other ingredients that you might not want. Fortunately, it's very easy to make your own chocolate candy. You can buy basic chocolate of different cocoa contents in special bakery stores or use the plain ready chocolate if you don't mind the additives. There are a few ways to melt chocolate, each with its pros and cons.

Double boiler (if you don't have one, use a bowl that's bigger than the pot): Put water in the bottom of the double boiler and chocolate pieces in the top. Gently heat the water and the chocolate will melt from the steam. Stir occasionally until the chocolate is completely melted. This method is quite quick, but it's important to make sure no steam, or water, gets into the bowl.

Microwave: Put chocolate pieces in a bowl and place in the microwave. Heat gently, in 10-second intervals, stirring in between. With this method, you don't need to worry about water and steam, but it's important to not overdo the heating as the chocolate burns easily.

And now for some fun!

1. Chocolate bars with nuts and other goodies

You need:

200 g high cocoa-percentage chocolate

Add one or more of the following (quantities according to taste):

toasted chopped nuts

coconut flakes

ground cinnamon

instant coffee powder

crushed hot pepper flakes

if you are not too sugar sensitive: chopped dried fruit

What to do:

1. Melt the chocolate as described on the previous page.
2. Add your flavoring and stir well.
3. Pour the mixture on baking paper and spread to desired thickness.
4. Let cool in the refrigerator.
5. Break into pieces.

▶ If you want even pieces; take the ready chocolate out of the refrigerator, leave it at room temperature for a few minutes and then cut with a sharp knife.

2. Ganache

You need:

200 g high cocoa-percentage chocolate

200 ml cream, dairy or coconut

For coating, use cocoa powder, coconut flakes, sesame seeds, or finely chopped nuts

Add one or more of the previous mentioned flavors and/or the following (quantities according to taste):

1-2 tbsp bourbon, whiskey, or flavored liquor (pay attention to the sugar content!)

a few drops of mint extract

What to do:

1. Prepare a pan with baking paper. It should go 2-3 cm up the sides of the pan.
2. Break the chocolate in a bowl.
3. Gently heat the cream in a pot until almost boiling (but don't let it boil), and pour over the chocolate pieces.
4. Let stand for a few minutes and then stir gently until all is mixed together.
5. Add your flavor and stir again.
6. Pour the mixture in the pan, about 2 cm high, and let cool in the refrigerator.
7. When stiff, cut squares with a sharp knife.

▶ For some fun, but messy, "extra," form each cube to a ball with your hands, and roll them in some coating.

3. Ice chocolate

A very good way to add coconut fat to your diet!

You need:

100 g chocolate of high cocoa-percentage

50-100 g coconut fat (more fat will give a softer consistency)

(Different flavorings as suggested in previous recipes)

What to do:

1. Prepare small candy paper cups on a tray or use an ice cube tray.
2. Melt coconut fat and chocolate together as described above.
3. Add flavoring, if desired, and stir well.
4. Pour 1-2 tsp of the mixture into the cups and refrigerate.

▶ Ice chocolates need to be kept refrigerated until served as they soften very quickly.

Chocolate spread

parve

When you start eating according to LCHF, you sometimes feel like you're going to miss out on all the sweet stuff. Eventually, when your taste buds get used to less sweet, you'll realize that there are plenty of "sweet" things to eat on your LCHF menu. But until then, it can be nice to have something candy-like to enjoy every now and then.

This chocolate spread is something I made up on the spur of the moment, and most people think it tastes like "Nutella."

You need:

roasted hazelnuts

cocoa powder

vanilla

some sweetener (optional)

a pinch of salt (optional)

What to do:

1. The easiest way to roast hazelnuts is to spread them on an oven pan and bake at low temperature (approximately 120° C/250° F) for 15-20 minutes. Stir every 5-10 minutes and at the same time check if the thin skin comes off easily. The nuts are ready when they start to be light brown and shell easy.

2. Remove the skins and put in a food processor. It doesn't matter if some of the skin is left.

3. Start grinding the nuts, stopping the food processor every few minutes to scrape down the sides with a spoon or rubber spatula, so that the nuts will be evenly chopped. Continue grinding until the nuts form a thick paste. (That happens when the oil starts to separate from the solids.)

4. Remove the paste from the mixer and put it in a bowl.

5. Add cocoa powder and vanilla to taste, and mix well.

Sometimes a few grains of salt will enhance the flavor (even the natural sweet flavor in the nuts and cocoa) but if you really want, add a tiny bit of sweetener to the mix.

▶ This chocolate spread can be refrigerated for quite a while, and is best enjoyed eaten with a spoon in small quantities.

6
BREADS, CAKES, COOKIES

BREADS, CAKES, COOKIES

Together with the "side dish dilemma," LCHF beginners frequently want something bread like, or cake like. At first, it may seem odd to use a slice of cheese or pastrami as a base, spread it with butter or mayonnaise and roll it up with a vegetable, instead of a sandwich. But believe me, it works as well.

In this chapter, I have gathered a few recipes for LCHF "breads," as well as a few cakes and cookies that you can use when you are celebrating something special.

Very quick breakfast rolls

dairy

This recipe I first found on a Swedish blog ("Lifezone" by Monique Forslund), but there are numerous variations. You'll find mine at the end. The best thing about this "bread," apart from being ready in no-time, is that my daughter even agreed to take it to school!

The recipe makes two rolls - no problem to freeze one for another time.

You need:

50 g (approximately 100 ml) ground almonds

25 g butter

1 egg

a pinch of salt

What to do:

1. Melt the butter in the microwave in a small bowl.
2. Add the ground almonds, egg, and salt and mix all together.
3. Divide the batter in two small bowls and cook in the microwave for 2 minutes at full power.
4. Take the "buns" out of the bowls and let them cool a little before cutting in halves to use.

My variation:

Quadruple the amounts!

1. Preheat the oven to 175° C / 345° F and line a baking pan with baking paper.
2. Melt the butter and mix it with the other ingredients in a bowl.
3. Add some spices such as oregano, garlic powder, dry onions, or cinnamon.
4. Spread the batter in the pan. It should be about 1 cm high.
5. Bake for about 15 minutes.

   Let cool, cut in squares and use as bread slices.

▶ This quadruple amount can also be used for a cake - exchange the salt for a little bit of sweetener, cut the sheet in half, layer with some cream or pudding in between, and also use some to cover the cake.

Breads, Cakes, Cookies

Auntie's cheesecake

dairy

My aunt has a cheesecake recipe that has become a real favorite in the extended family. Even without actual cream or lemon zest in the original recipe, it's creamy and a little bit tart, and now I've adapted it to LCHF.

You Need:

250 g cream cheese (unsalted)

1 egg

1 ½ tsp psyllium husk

1 tbsp sweetener

100 ml sour cream

Topping:

200 ml sour cream

1 tsp vanilla

1 tbsp sweetener

What to do:

1. Preheat the oven to 200° C/ 390° F.
2. Make the crust according to the "sweet pie crust" recipe (page 132) and prebake for 10 minutes.
3. Mix the filling ingredients in a bowl.
4. Pour the batter in the crust.
5. Bake for about 20 minutes, until the cake is stable but hasn't started to brown.
6. Take the cake out of the oven and turn up the heat as high as possible (250-275° C/480-525° F).
7. Mix the ingredients for the topping.
8. Pour the topping on the cake and bake for about 5 minutes.
9. Take the cake out of the oven and let cool.

   It's actually easier to serve if you leave the cake in the refrigerator overnight.

- Serve with freshly brewed coffee. You can also add some (pureed) berries on the side.
- By the way, Hubby says the best way to cut cheesecake is with dental floss.

Chocolate cookies

dairy, parve

These are simple cookies that can be made dairy or parve - simple but still very rich in flavor, simple but can be varied in different ways.
A batch makes about 30 small cookies.

You need:

75 g butter or coconut fat

150 g ground almonds

2 ½ tbsp cocoa powder

approximately 1 tbsp honey

1 tsp vanilla essence

1 egg white

What to do:

1. Preheat the oven to 200° C/390° F.
2. Soften the fat and mix all the ingredients together.
3. With the help of two spoons, form cookies and drop onto a cookie sheet.
4. Bake for 10-12 minutes.

▶ For more chewy cookies, chop in some raisins.

▶ For more crunchy cookies, chop in some nuts.

▶ For the "lazy" - spread the dough in a pan and bake. Cut in squares.

▶ You can also roll the batter in baking paper or aluminum foil to make a sausage. Put in the freezer for use later. Thaw slightly and cut in slices to bake.

Cinnamon cookies

dairy, parve

These cookies are as chewy as oatmeal cookies, and it's the Fibrex that does it. The cookies can of course be made with or without raisins. Makes about 25 cookies.

You need:

100 g butter or coconut fat

150 g ground almonds

35 g Fibrex

1 tsp ground cinnamon

approximately 1 tbsp honey

1 egg white

20 g small or chopped raisins (optional)

What to do:

1. Preheat the oven to 200° C / 390° F.
2. Soften the fat and mix all the ingredients together.
3. Roll the batter in baking paper or aluminum foil to make a sausage and put in the fridge for 1-2 hours.
4. Cut 4-5 mm slices and place them on a cookie sheet.
5. Bake for 10 to 12 minutes.

▶ You can also prepare the cookie dough without the cinnamon and instead sprinkle cinnamon on top of the cut slices before baking.

Oopsies

dairy

It's great for when you just "have to" put your butter and cheese on something.

The name "Oopsie," I heard, originates from a recipe by Dana Carpender. She was making this low-carb "bread" and by mistake doubled one of the ingredients but not the other. It came out even better and the Oopsie was born.

Since then, different people have made their own variations. Here I bring the recipe I found, with my variations at the end; use it to make a jelly-roll or as an alternative pizza crust!

You need:

3 eggs

100 g cream cheese (use unsalted cheese for a jellyroll!)

a pinch of salt

½ tbsp psyllium husk, will give it a "spongier" texture (optional)

½ tsp baking powder (optional)

- ▶ for a pizza bottom: add ground herbs such as oregano or basil
- ▶ for a jelly-roll, double the amounts and exchange the salt for a sweetener

What to do:

1. Preheat the oven to 150° C / 300° F.
2. Separate the eggs.
3. Put the whites in a bowl, add the salt, and whip till stiff.
4. Mix the yolks with the cream cheese in another bowl. Add psyllium husk and/or baking powder if using.
5. Carefully fold the whipped whites into the yolk batter.
6. Spoon the mixture onto a baking sheet and bake for 20-30 minutes, until golden.

- ▶ For pizza: spread the batter in the pan and bake for about 15 minutes. Remove from the oven, spread tomato sauce, cheese, and topping and bake for another 15 minutes or until the cheese melts.

- ▶ For a jelly-roll, spread the batter in the pan and bake. Let cool, add filling (some whipped cream and berries, or vanilla/cinnamon cream cheese) and roll it up.

Pie crust - sweet

dairy, parve

This is a very easy pie crust that can be used for either baked or cold fillings. You can also vary the nuts, according to your preference, or add some cocoa powder or just chopped dark chocolate to make the crust richer.

You need:

200 g ground almonds

1 tbsp sweetener

1 egg

50 g melted butter or coconut fat

1 tbsp vanilla

What to do:

1. Preheat the oven to 175° C / 345° F.
2. Mix the dry ingredients.
3. Add the melted fat and the egg.
4. Using your palm, press the dough into a baking pan, including up the sides.

▶ For a baked filling: prebake the crust for about 10 minutes, fill the crust and continue baking.

▶ For a non-baked filling: bake the crust for 20 to 25 minutes or till golden, let cool and fill.

Pie crust – savory

dairy, parve

This is, in a way, similar to the sweet pie crust, but actually it is its very own recipe.

Vary the nut mixture according to the filling:
- Mostly almonds for a tuna pie.
- Exchange about 1/3 of the almonds with chopped walnuts for a creamy cheese pie.
- Add some coarsely chopped roasted hazelnuts for a meat pie.

You need:

175 ml ground almonds

50 g flaxseeds

1 egg

50 g melted butter or coconut fat

What to do:

1. Preheat the oven to 175° C/345° F.
2. Mix the dry ingredients.
3. Add the melted fat and the egg.
4. Press into a baking pan, including up the sides.
5. Prebake for about 10 minutes.
6. Add the filling and finish baking.

Za'atar bread

dairy, parve

Slice it and toast it!
And you can of course exchange the za'atar with other interesting spices like garlic, cumin, anise or fennel.

You need:

7 eggs

75 g melted butter or coconut fat

50 g almond flour

50 g coconut flour

1 tsp baking powder

½ tsp salt

1 tbsp ground za'atar

What to do:

1. Preheat the oven to 160° C/320° F and grease a loaf pan. (Or put baking paper in the pan.)
2. Mix the dry ingredients in a bowl.
3. Add the eggs and the fat and stir well.
4. Pour the batter into the loaf pan.
5. Bake for about 40 minutes until the bread gets a nice light brown color.
6. Take the pan out of the oven and let cool.

▶ Serve with butter, cheese, and a cup of tea.

www.ingramcontent.com/pod-product-compliance
Lightning Source LLC
Chambersburg PA
CBHW040052160426
43192CB00002B/44